TSUNAMI vs. the FUKUSHIMA 50

TSUNAMI vs. the FUKUSHIMA 50

poems   Lee Ann Roripaugh

MILKWEED EDITIONS

Published 2019 by Milkweed Editions
Printed in the United States of America
Cover design by Mary Austin Speaker
Cover artwork by Chie Yoshii: *Dragon*. Oil on wood panel.
Author photo by Cathy Flum
19 20 21 22 23 5 4 3 2 1
First Edition

Milkweed Editions, an independent nonprofit publisher, gratefully acknowledges sustaining support from the Ballard Spahr Foundation; the Jerome Foundation; the McKnight Foundation; the National Endowment for the Arts; the Target Foundation; and other generous contributions from foundations, corporations, and individuals. Also, this activity is made possible by the voters of Minnesota through a Minnesota State Arts Board Operating Support grant, thanks to a legislative appropriation from the arts and cultural heritage fund, and a grant from Wells Fargo. For a full listing of Milkweed Editions supporters, please visit milkweed.org.

Library of Congress Cataloging-in-Publication Data

Names: Roripaugh, Lee Ann, author.
Title: Tsunima vs. the Fukushima 50 : poems / Lee Ann Roripaugh.
Description: First edition. | Minneapolis, Minnesota : Milkweed Editions, 2019.
Identifiers: LCCN 2018033636 (print) | LCCN 2018034332 (ebook) | ISBN
   9781571319494 (ebook) | ISBN 9781571314857 (pbk. : alk. paper)
Classification: LCC PS3568.O717 (ebook) | LCC PS3568.O717 A6 2019 (print) |
   DDC 811/.54—dc23
LC record available at https://lccn.loc.gov/2018033636

Milkweed Editions is committed to ecological stewardship. We strive to align our book production practices with this principle, and to reduce the impact of our operations in the environment. We are a member of the Green Press Initiative, a nonprofit coalition of publishers, manufacturers, and authors working to protect the world's endangered forests and conserve natural resources. *tsunami vs. the fukushima 50* was printed on acid-free 30% postconsumer-waste paper by Versa Press.

This book is a tribute to, in memory and honor of, the victims and survivors of the 2011 Tohoku earthquake and tsunami, and the subsequent Fukushima Daiichi nuclear disaster.

For heroes, both visible and invisible.

For the ferocity of women. May we all survive and rise.

For the troubled legacies and unexpected gifts of trauma: the wounds and the superpowers, the hypervigilance, the Mothra-like antennae.

For Kundiman, beautiful poetry tribe.

For sisters, chosen family, and friends: Emily Haddad, Cathy Flum, Susan Wolfe, Pen Pearson, Caroline Hong, Allison Adelle Hedge Coke, Lindy Obach, Bridget Jacobs, Katy Beem, Natanya Ann Pulley, and Darlene Farabee, among many others, with love.

For all of my many wonderful colleagues and students at the University of South Dakota, the University of Nebraska MFA in Writing, and the Carlow University MFA in Writing, with much gratitude for your inspiration and community.

For all of the mentors, editors, journals, presses, and reading venues who have supported my work over the years with such kindness and generosity—including a special thanks to Daniel Slager and the entire staff of Milkweed Editions.

For Nobu, Aiko, Nanami, Kuzuri, Yuki, Tampopo, Genji, Muku, Kenji, Ten-chan, and Kumo.

And, with love always, for Bruce, my sweet giant, who fills the cracks with gold.

contents

When man falls into conflict with nature,
monsters are born.
—*The Return of Godzilla* (1985)

TSUNAMI vs. the FUKUSHIMA 50

ontology of tsunami

awoken venom

cobra come uncharmed

glittering rush
of fanged lightning
that strikes
and strikes again

tsunami has no name

call her the scalded splash
of tea jarred from
a broken cup's cracked glaze

call her the blood-soaked shirt
and cutaway pants
pooled ruby on the floor / rising biohazard

ill-omened oil that stills
the wings of birds

she spills
and spills
and spills over

a sloshed bucket
tipped-over pitcher

the bent tin cup's
cool sluice of rinse
poured over skin's
delicious prickle

ginger's cleansing sting
erasing the soft flesh of fish
from the tongue

she goes by no name

call her *annihilatrix*

call her *tabula rasa*

she's the magic slate's
crackling cellophane page

shellacked wings un-clung
from staticky black elytra

the liminal torn-open, turning
words into invisible birds lifting
unruly as catastrophe

yes, but / and . . .

(if only, if only—
meticulous swift precision
of disaster's Swiss watch)

she remains unnamed

call her the *meme*
infecting your screen

call her the *malware*
gone viral

dreaming tsunami

maybe she was sleeping:
a dream of fishes helixed
in spiraling schools
anemone's veronicas
ouroboros of sea snakes
the chambered nautilus's
slow-whorled tornadoes

(*hypnosis of dust motes*)

girl in the grass face down
soiled focus, brain's green blur
lens wheezing in and out
of tiny myopias: ant, gnat,
midge, aphid, no-see-um
Nanking cherry petals'
sickened swirl / snapdragons'
red mouths pinched open
to the waking dream
from which she can't awaken

(*hypnosis of dust motes*)

mosquito stuck in her ear
too scared to tell / can't hear
above the buzzing
ambered seal of earwax
fevering one side of her face

she drowns at night
in deep cold sweat / dreams
she's a sea monster

(*hypnosis of dust motes / dead calm*)

where are the fault lines
she hides along the floorboards?

what happens when she wakens
from this clam before the thorn?

tsunami goes to canada

she liked the clouds
which coasted down close
spoke to her sotto voce
in the glamorous
language of nebulizers

go away they seemed
to breathe (though not *unkindly*)
before sucking her deeper in

she stared smitten
at the mountains / stricken
afflicted by them
besotted in the lunch room
with an unquenchable crush

though maybe she worried too much
about bears / about pepper spray

the falls gave her strange ideas
about froth
and glitter
and churn
and spume
and spill

maybe someday she would pull back
and let it all go to fall like that

a silvery levering of pachinko balls

a cat vomiting from a great height

perched swirl of vertigo lurching
on the mountainside switchback

no taking back the swoon

animal portents foretell the rise of tsunami

when elephants kneel
pressing their trunks
down to the ground
like seismic antennae

when mole rats head-drum
adumbrations / listen for
predictions / augured jawbones
snugged to tunnel walls

when cats spill from windows
slip through opened doors
some welder's torch sizzle
fizzing the tips of their whiskers

when insect swarms clot the shore
in a frantic tangled macramé
and hippopotamuses bellow
a chorus of mournful cellos

when snakes awaken
from hibernation / curlicuing
up from their dens
like bolts come unscrewed—
their frozen bodies
a semiology of hieroglyphs
in the snow:

実行してください離れて速く
津波が来ています。
非常に大規模な 1 つがここに向かっています。
危険にさらされています。

when double helixes spun by skeins
of flying sparrows unravel

when centipedes appear
in rippling synchronicities

when colonies of toads erupt
like burst popcorn
from ponds' silver foil

when fish come unschooled

when bees abandon their queens
flee their honey

when silky clusters of bats lift
in smoky volcanic furies as if

rising / from a city ravished / in flame

radioactive man

the papers started calling me
Radioactive Man after tests from
the Japan Aerospace Exploration Agency
revealed the highest radiation levels
in anyone they'd ever screened

I guess I'm the champion, I joke
to reporters who come for interviews
like visitors from another planet

bulky and brightly awkward
in white hazmat suits, they look
like mourners at a Buddhist funeral

and so I light a cigarette to dangle
from the corner of my lip and grin

even eight miles away, in Tomioka,
the sound of Reactor 4 exploding
was completely unmistakable,
so I took my elderly parents south
to my aunt in Iwaki, who refused
to even open her door to us because
she said we were contaminated

then we tried a temporary shelter
but it was full, so we came home
again to the no go zone, and when

other relatives agreed to take in
my parents, I stayed behind
to care for the abandoned animals

I've seen many terrible things:
cages filled with withered songbirds,
horses left to starve in their stalls,
an abandoned puppy that grew
too big for the chain around its neck

I rescue as many as I can:
the dog trapped inside a barn

for months, who survived by eating
the dead flesh of starved cattle

or the feral ostrich so vicious
the police who border patrol
the nuclear exclusion zone
armed with Geiger counters
nicknamed her The Boss

all over Tomioka, the animals
recognize the sound of my truck,
and come running to meet me
when I make my daily rounds

many come to stay with me
at my family's old rice farm

living without water
or electricity in the ruins
of the town where I was born
is sometimes very lonely

I wait for cancer or leukemia
and joke to The Boss about
becoming a superhero through
a radioactive ostrich bite

sometimes I think of visiting
my two kids, who live
with my ex-wife in Tokyo,
but then I remind myself
of the invisible dust coated
in cesium particles that's in
my clothes, my hair, my skin

I remember I can see my future
in the sick animals I care for

in the American *Watchmen* comics,
Dr. Manhattan was once tricked
into believing he'd given everyone
he ever loved cancer, through
exposure to his radioactive body

just the thought of this undid him,
made him feel so solitary and blue
he left the earth behind for eons,
to brood in exile on the moon

hungry tsunami / tsunami as galactus

the hunger of trying to hold back
the hunger a little bit longer

the hunger of restraint and pullback
churn and growl of beached fishes
in an agitated bouillabaisse
liquid silver squirming on an empty shore

to lick the gilding from the buildings
like golden drizzles of caramel

to take the cake / flick off the crumbs

to raze the fruit / spit out the pits

the hunger of sucked-out marrow
the unwillingly pried-open oyster
the cracked and pillaged lobster claw

to shuck / to husk / to unshell
her way to what's most tender

to dismantle the protective scrims
that signal a cache of rawness

to demolish defenseless succulence

the hunger for the liquid center
squirt of ganache in a swiss truffle
chocolate lava cake's molten fondant core

to feed past the end of greed

to feast past the end of want

to gorge past the borders of voraciousness
until she becomes the monstrous goddess
of binge / pure mercenary lack

the blooded face

blood in the water

the blood moon's exposed sweet throat
with its lipsticked jugular bitten clean out

mothra flies again

I knew it was a bad omen
when silk moth cocoons hung
unhatched like stillborn husks
from the mulberry trees—
imagoes furled tight as parasols
crumbling to ash and dust inside

but still, I felt so lucky
to have survived the tsunami

I felt so lucky to be alive
after three reactor meltdowns

daijobu, said mayor Norio Kanno

daijobu, echoed the village officials

everything was fine, fine, fine

for weeks, everything was *daijobu*
while our village was irradiated:
the soil, the water, the produce,
the dust particles, the rain

three months later, Iitate
was a ghost town crumbling
to dust, infested with mold

and vermin, and we had become
part of the nuclear diaspora

now we stay in prefab shelters
assigned to us in Date City,
waiting for cleanup workers
to scrape off Iitate's farmland
topsoil—sealing it into bags
no one wants to handle,
like too-hot sweet potatoes

and when the high-pressure washers
that were promised never arrived,
the workers began scrubbing off
contaminants using only paper towels

how can we ever go back there?

at night I lie awake and unpack
my worries like wooden *kokeshi* dolls,
nested one inside the other

what if? what if? what if?
my heart clangs inside my chest,
then waits with held breath
for the twin girls nested inside me
to shift or twist or kick in reply
within their amniotic fluid

I try not to think of the cocoons
shriveling on the vine, the weeks
I unknowingly exposed my twins,
small as a pair of Bing cherries,
to radioactive contamination while
believing everything was *daijobu*

instead, I get up and watch
late-night *kaiju* movies on television,
the ones my father used to love

all of the monsters rising
one by one on monster island:
Gojira, Radon, Gigan, Ebirah

last week, I saw a movie
about *Hedora*, the smog monster,
who fell to earth from outer space
in a cloud of toxic spores,
while tonight I doze on the sofa
as *Mosura* is summoned by her
twin fairy priestesses, who sing
for her when they're in danger

how fiercely she defends them
with her electric beam antennae,
her deadly lightning bolts,
the scatter of poisonous yellow
shed from the scales on her wings

when I wake the light is harsh,
my neck a sore bent stem,
and the red ambulance melody
of my *Shobijin*, my small beauties,
sirens a distress call inside me:

mosura ya mosura
tasukete yo te yobeba
toki o koete
umi o koete
name no yo ni yatte kuru
mamorigami

shapeshifter tsunami: a scary epithalamium

they're the glitter of koi
snake's chain-mail slink / heart-shaped
cockle belly dragging
as they Facebook creep
on tiger's hushed paws
velvet-horned / oxen-eared
shy-eyed as a rabbit until
camel's spit and eagle's claw

they gender-switch easy as
the sea change shimmer
of lenticular flicker pictures
flipping with each shift of light:
mtf / ftm / sea walnuts
to Venus's girdles / emperors
and clownfish / sea stars
or the beautiful moon wrasse

sometimes they pass as human
buy laundry detergent
forget which day's trash day
update the Netflix queue / quietly
read Godzilla comix on the plane

sometimes they take a bride/groom
and adopt a kitten from the pound
until they begin to turn invisible

secretly start smoking again / exhalations
of clouds and ash on the back porch

newly single / monster's their go-to form
glitter and hiss and growl and spit and claw

the dragon tattoos of firemen
a talisman against burning
calling in their quenching
tonnage of water to shore

the resolute voice of Miki Endo
dragon's turtle messenger
calling out loudspeakered warnings
calling the silvery fury in

they're the kind of dragon who'll
demolish town hall / pluck out
the lone girl still manning
the disaster prevention office
to keep as their own choice pearl

they're the kind of dragon who'll
tear the world apart / toppling
institutions and tossing cars
troubling the nuclear reactor
down to its cracked fragile core

they're the kind of dragon who
won't stop until they've unrepressed
the phoenix who dreams inside them
becoming their own mortal enemy
birthing their own monster bride

the nuptial bed's self-immolation

honeymoon's toxic / apocalypse of flame

miki endo as flint marko (a.k.a. sandman)

after the tsunami took me
I was both here and not here

I mean I was everywhere,
but also nowhere all at once

does this seem strange to you?

it used to seem strange to me
but now it's just how things are

at first, I concentrated very hard
on trying to see my feet, to know
if I was a ghost or not, but when
sneakers filled with foot bones
began to surface in the Pacific,
I stopped thinking these thoughts

all during the tsunami, I held to
my post at the disaster center,
calling out evacuation orders
on the loudspeaker, warning
people to seek higher ground

warning everyone to run away!

I still feel that terrible siren
swirling around in a loud howl

inside me, but now scattered
like radioactive sand rinsed
by a high tide, the temple
rock garden's spiral and whorl
erased by the brooms of monks

as a child, I once saw a swarm
of ladybugs crawling over something

from a distance it looked like
an encrustation of orange M&M's

up close, the orange shells
climbing and clambering in constant
jumbled motion, one sometimes falling
to end up stranded on its back

the frantic scramble of hairpin legs

occasionally, a shell might crack
itself open into a sizzled glimpse
of crinkly tissue-paper wings

I was scared to think about what
could be hiding beneath
this living armor of marching orange

maybe only a piece of rotted wood,
or perhaps an abandoned vegetable

but what if it was something once
vulnerable, downy, and warm?

something severed or stillborn?

something with pulse and blood
and breath bitten right out of it?

and even though I didn't really
want to know, I poked at it
with a twig, startling beetles
into a metallic explosion of sparks

like a thrown-down bag of bang snaps

like tiny bright castanets flying away

maybe you are now wondering
about what the something was
that was hidden underneath?

it was nothing . . .

I mean, nothing was *there* there

just absence and hollow,
which scared me most of all

now I keep trying to assemble
my dissembling self
atom by painful split atom

my microscopic shifting wakens
the snakes, and makes uneasy
the schooled dreams of fish

I cluck my tongue and maybe
you hear it echoed in the clicked
ticking of the Geiger counter

sometimes I find myself hiding inside
a hibernating tsunami siren, paralyzed
and mute—my throat a raw ache
of silenced night terrors—trying
to wake and unquiet myself free

tsunami battles the pink robots / french poststructuralist tsunami

it's such a pitiful bukkake
those post-tsunami Roombas

cooling downplant walls
stripping off paint

and concrete surface
with their waterjets

(Hitachi's "Arounder"
Mitsubishi's "MEISTeR"

the diesel-fueled
"ASTACO-SoRa")

but hers / is still bigger
than theirs / mythological

slippery and apocryphal
as Butler's lesbian phallus

she doesn't give a shit
about the ring of pee

crescenting the toilet
or if the hamper

overflows, she's a hoarder
and slob, deconstructing

the domestic (symbolic) order
of the melted-down core

with the fluid roller-ball
cursive of jellyfish

the spilled milk ink
of octopus and squid

the squirted rush
of salt and brine

unbolting the bolts
unscrewing the screws

oh tin men, she laughs
and laughs at you

with her gulls and crazed
seaweed hair / rusting down

your hearts to orange filing
and cringing flake

tick tock / tick / tock
until they all / stop

year of the hitachi snake

forked fiberscopic tongue
sixth-sensing irradiated air

it is equipped with Createc's
N-visage cameras and three-
dimensional imaging software

among the zodiac signs
snakes are highly intuitive

metal snakes demonstrate
an appreciation for luxury
and state of the art goods

it shape-shifts into a u-form

snakes are suspicious
and prefer to work alone

programmed to shimmy down
the reactor core, identify
the configuration of melted
fuel rods fallen to the bottom
of the containment chamber

following the probe, it will be
dangerously radioactive

like a cyborg Kiyohime,
the spurned snake woman,
searching for Anchin,
the handsome priest she loved

snakes are beautiful
but vain and high-tempered

when Kiyohime shape-
shifted into her snake form
Anchin hid from her wrath
under the Dojoji Temple bell

it will be retired and stored—
lustrous and glowing—inside
a shielded box for centuries

the heat of Kiyohime's
rage burned and melted
the bronze bell, along with
Anchin, hidden beneath it

snakes are known to be possessive

after the new bell arrived
Kiyohime's spirit remained
coiled around the bell, forcing
the priests at Dojoji Temple
to perform an exorcism

bell come unrung:

Kiyohime left the temple
and fled to the Hidaka River

300 tons of contaminated water
leaking into the ocean every day

beautiful tsunami

it's no secret she's a little bit vain

vain in the way reptiles are vain

a 10-story building's worth of solipsism

with her head full of snakes
that paralytic stare

coconut palms and mangroves tricked up
along the shoreline don't slow her down

sea walls can't stop her

labyrinths of floodgates won't fool her
into siphoning away her power

she's a mega-tsunami of pure hubris
cross-dressed in high femme
splashy / shiny / crystalline
all liquid curve and fluid light

with her Hello Kitty barrettes
pink glitter ribbons furbelowing
all that snaky girlzilla hair

bored now, she pouts in her little girl voice
before it all goes to shit

RAAAHRRR!!! she hollers

SKREEEEEE!!! she thrashes her tail

HRRRRRRR . . . she thrums pensively

bullets and fireballs and even atomic blasts
can't stop her

she wants to smash it all to bits
easy-peasy as a spurned lover
sweeping cutlery and crockery
off the restaurant table

the brilliantine petulant clatter of it

fuck the puny villagers
with their tiny flaming matchsticks!

fuck the helicopters she swats
away like lethargic flies!

fuck those candy-shelled tanks
the marching termite armies!

send in the Smog Monster!

summon Mothra!

bring on Gidora!

as if / the mirror stage
of her own monstrosity
might make her recoil

call in the Mechatsunami!

as if / the feedback loop
of her cyborg doppelganger
might give her pause

when instead:

she surfaces like a terrible fish

rises like the Dark Phoenix

comes in for the kiss like Narcissus

hulk smash

because it was afternoon
and I was at the carnation farm
when the earthquake struck

because by the time I arrived
back home to help my family
traffic jams had clogged shut
the main arterial roads leading
inland from Futaba-machi

because when the tsunami
breached the sea wall,
and concrete disintegrated like
strewn chunks of soggy plywood,
we had to leave our car
and flee for higher ground

because the elevated hill
marked as the evacuation point
for an elementary school
seemed like it should be safe,
until the tsunami rose like
a thundering wall of water
and blotted out the sky

because there wasn't time
for us to climb all the way

up the hill, so I held my wife
and daughter in my arms,
and we clung together tightly
wrapped around a tree

because the icy water
uprooted the tree so easily,
like plucking up a blade
of grass, and tore my wife
Mayumi away from me

because I could see Natsu
was crying for her mother,
though I couldn't hear her

above the roar of the water,
and I was scared I'd hurt her
from holding on so tight

because when I regained
consciousness again with
a concussion and a broken leg
after having blacked out,
my arms were empty

because she was only three

because I was taken against
my will to a hospital in Iitate,
where I was promised that

rescue workers would search
the coast for any survivors
and bring them to safety

because the meltdowns
and hydrogen explosions
at Fukushima Daiichi began
the next day and everyone
within a 20-kilometer radius
was evacuated, so that
no one was able to look for
my wife or my daughter

because the nuclear accident
at Fukushima Daiichi was,
as it turns out, preventable

because what if my wife
and daughter were injured,
but still alive, and what if
someone had only searched
for them during those early
days after the tsunami?

because it was over a month
before I was allowed back
into the exclusion zone,
where I found Mayumi's
body in a nearby rice field

because my wife's remains
were so terribly decomposed
after having been left out
to weather the elements, insects,
birds, and vermin, she was
no longer recognizable,
and the Buddhist burial rites
could not be followed
before her body was burned

because over four years
have passed with my life still
in limbo, unable to return
to what's left of my home,
to my work breeding carnations,
unable to lay Mayumi's ashes
to rest on ancestral grounds

because my daughter Natsu
is still missing, even though
I search for her every month
in the five-hour increments
allowed by radiation guidelines

because I am by nature
a quiet and scientific man,
a botanist by trade, but
I work so ferociously at
clearing debris and digging
along the shoreline in search

of my daughter's remains—
tearing off my hazmat gear
when it gets in the way,
or when it becomes too hot—
that volunteer search teams
have nicknamed me The Hulk

because so what, I no longer
care about being exposed
to radiation, and maybe
it'll make me stronger anyway,
like the weird profusion
of too-bright and hardy flowers

blooming in the irradiated wake
of Hiroshima and Nagasaki . . .
maybe even strong enough
to hold on to what matters.

because plans are underway
to build a containment facility
in Futaba City for the bags
upon bags of contaminated topsoil
and radioactive debris gathered
by the cleanup workers that
no one knows what to do with

because if this happens
Futaba will become just
a permanent trash site

for nuclear waste, a toxic
garbage dump, where
my daughter's remains
will be abandoned forever

because how can I let this be?

because my arms are empty

because she was only three

because now, every month
when I spend my five hours
searching the no go zone,
and I see one of the many
rusted TEPCO signs reading
*Nuclear Power: Bright Future
of Energy*, I feel such a huge
surge of adrenaline and rage,
that I have to tear it down

tsunami as misguided kwannon

her hypervigilance such that
everything becomes a piercing
a harrowing she can't turn off

her superpower a wound
a lightning rod / and sponge / speaking
the language of wounds to wounds

like echolocation that dopplers
the contours of another's sorrow
against her own ricocheted song

or touch subtle as the naked push broom
of a star-nosed mole's tentacles
nuzzling the bruised flesh of worms

or a nose for muscling out fresh blood
old ghosts / the sweet fat of lost dreams
like a winter-lean bear come spring

or feathery antennae's raw quiver
pinched to ash by the hot sparks
of disconsolate pheromones

her nervous system a glitter
of neurotransmitters on fire

an electric-chaired switchboard
short-circuited / fuse blown

she's the exposed nerve:

exuviated snake / hulled bean
husked cicada / chaffed seed
peeled grape / shucked clam

she's the conduit / aperture / cracked
mirror to all that's scintillant and broken

until her compassion mushroom clouds
and swells like a fever / a red infection
a rising tide of salt tears
for the world's fractured core

how could she possibly stop herself
from sweeping it all into her broken cradle
to soothe and rock and weep over?

(her fingers itchy to pilfer and spare
what's plush and tender
like the rabbit stolen by the moon)

how could she possibly stop herself
from the mercy of washing it all clean
in her terrible estuary of lamentations?

white tsubame

after the *tsubame* disappeared,
white feathers started sprouting
from my shoulders and back
in a furious itch of stiff follicles,
the weird tickle of snowy down

it all began when more and more
damaged butterflies appeared
with stunted or crumpled wings

and the stained glass windows
of cicadas' wings turned into
a tangled lace mesh crocheted
by a bent, contaminated hook

soon the hypnotic thrum
and drone pulsing the horizon
during late summer nights
fell silent: no power-tool surge
of cicadas, no squeak-shined
scrubbing or tambourine jingle
from the katydids and crickets

the *gwa gwa gwa* of frogs
stopped from invisible ponds

and even towns just outside
the nuclear exclusion zone

became ghost towns, too,
when barn swallows lost
all of their blues, turning
into albino ghosts, before
abandoning their mud nests
tucked under house eaves,
leaving them to decay until
all of the birdsong was gone
and everything was irradiated
by a blinding wash of silence

my parents begged me
to tell no one about
the white swallow wings
feathering my back

my father worked for TEPCO
cleaning up radioactive topsoil
in the no go zone
and didn't want any trouble

my mother was worried
I'd be shunned as damaged,
so she bound down
my wings every morning
until they ached under gauze
and I felt crumpled
and stunted as one of
the deformed butterflies,
or the pruned-down bonsai

my grandfather in Ukedo
trained to grow into
strange transfigurations

before my grandfather
disappeared during the tsunami
I visited him every year
during *amba matsuri*—
the festival of the safe wave

I loved how he split open
fresh salmon with a silver
fish knife to squeeze out
sticky orange roe directly
onto hot rice for breakfast

now coastal fishing boats
rock crippled in their harbors,
crumpled sails pinned down,
going on fake runs, only
so scientists can test
for cesium levels in the fish

my wings grow larger
and more unwieldy, become
difficult for me to hide
underneath my hoody

sometimes I stand on the roof
of the tallest building

in Minamisoma and think that
if I jumped, then everyone
would finally know the truth

barn swallows are said
to be harbingers of luck
so maybe I could be like
the *tsubame* who returns,
bearing good fortune

I could fly across the river
looping over water
bright with the hot swirl
of irradiated golden carp

I could fly all the way
across the border patrols
into the no go zone

I could fly all the way
back to Ukedo to search
for my missing grandfather
because ever since
the insects died off
and stopped their singing,
I can hear his lost
and desecrated bones
tapping out an SOS
into the too-quiet nights:

please help me
I am lost

please help me
I am lost

tsunami grrlsplains allergies

fuck taupe, she says:
milquetoasty blood cells
band-aiding faux infections

whitewashing the body's narrative
spinning a tail to wag the dog

anaphylaxis with shellfish
the superhyper bowl of peanuts

a gorgeous explosion
of mold spores like cosmic glitter
in the bloodstream:
alternaria, aspergillus,
cladosporium, and *penicillium*

allergens barbarians
at the gate melting down
the candy shell
of the nuclear power plant's
chocolate core

did you know taupe's
French vague
for the color of moles?

which might be brownish-grey
or grayish-brown

or sometimes pinkish
as in rose taupe
or mauve taupe
or faux taupe

immune system's false hope
against REM and mSv

so just gloss over it
paint it all taupe

duct tape shut the doors

wait for the frantic
castanet clicking
of Geiger counters:

Three Mile Island
Chernobyl
Fukushima Daiichi

duck and cover

stick your head
in the sand
to glow
and smolder
and strobe

anonymous, as invisible man

I agree to speak, but only
on condition of anonymity

I worry about my children
being ostracized at school
and still feel much shame
for being unable to prevent
over 150 thousand people
having to flee their homes
in the nuclear exclusion zone

it happened so quickly, like
a line of falling dominos, one tile
knocking down the next:
first, the terrible jolts
of the Tohoku earthquake
causing the massive tsunami,
which knocked out power
and flooded the emergency
generators, preventing coolants
from reaching the fuel rods,
causing them to overheat
and melt down three
of the nuclear reactors, leading
to the hydrogen explosions

a hero? I don't consider myself a hero

the international media
named us the Fukushima 50
but there were hundreds
of engineers, technicians
soldiers, and firefighters
who remained in the heart
of the disaster for weeks
with dwindling food and water
and no reinforcements

those of us who responded
to plant manager Yoshida's call
and returned to Fukushima Daiichi
to cool the crippled reactors
by manually pumping in seawater
were prepared to sacrifice
our lives like kamikaze pilots

the other workers formed a line
and saluted us as we departed
the disaster-response headquarters
where we'd been evacuated

TEPCO reprimanded Yoshida
for defying their orders,
then later commended him
for preventing a chain
of nuclear fission reactions
that would have led
to the evacuation of Tokyo

some people claimed we saved Japan

it was a full month before
I'd leave Fukushima Daiichi again,
and when I was finally released
for the first time to visit my family,
I was almost unrecognizable

I'd lost so much weight
and grown a scraggly beard

I hadn't bathed in weeks

I was asked to strip down
for the compulsory radiation check
and given a too-big track suit,
a plastic bag to carry my things

I decline to reveal
my internal radiation levels

people gave me strange looks
on the train and avoided
sitting next to me, but when
we arrived at Tokyo station
the city glittered and jostled
the same as before Fukushima,
as if none of it had happened

I got off the train, slipping
into the city's stream . . .
and then I quietly disappeared

tsunami's debris

her terrible radiance

snaking in a clockwise gyre
spiraling the North Pacific

pulverized cities flung back
to water like sprinkled *furikake*

her radio-waved wake
an awful flower blossoming

what sinks sinks / what floats floats

snarled tangle fronding the comb's
tooth of Midway's atoll

plastic bits clogged in the snag
of the garbage patch

she's an unsubtle thief
a cryptic giver of gifts:

All Joy Air Freshener's
diaspora of aerosol cans

a boy's lucky soccer ball
head-butted from the waves

Harley-Davidson wrecked
on the shores of British Columbia

Misawa Port's 165-ton dock
washed up on Oregon's Agate Beach
studded with the tiny garnish
of a stowaway Japanese starfish

Ryo un Maru / empty ghost ship's
uncanny drifting across the Pacific
into the Gulf of Alaska
like a child's paper boat

Ryo un Maru / good-luck ship
machine-gunned down
by a coast guard cutter
into scuttled blaze and flame

running shoes swift with bones
marathoning the waves
because everyone knows a ghost
is a ghost if it has no feet

heralds for colonies / of ghosts to come:

a bloat of oyster buoys
a landfill of washing machines
a traffic jam of cars
an armada of ghost ships
a siege of rubber ducks

her terrible radiance

mushroom spore / dandelion seed

shells of nebulae / shed by a supernova

what belongs to you / doesn't

in the shattered absence
of an unraveling cosmos

what tiny bits of debris will you
unexpectedly ache for?

what small particles will you
cling to / as if you actually could?

ama, the woman of the sea

how the tourists loved to see us
diving for wild abalone and sea urchin
in our traditional white *isogi*, with
wooden buoys tethered to our waists
for when we surfaced to rest

in my prime, I could hold my breath
for three minutes before releasing
the pent-up air in my lungs
in a long gasping *isobue*—
those hyperventilated whistles
of the *ama* ricocheting across
the bay like the sighs of ghosts

when I first became an *ama*
I was just a teenager, and we dove
naked, wearing only a loincloth
and a *tenugui* to cover our hair

a photographer once visited
my tiny fishing village to capture
pictures of *ama* at work, and now
there is a black-and-white image
of me as a "Japanese mermaid"
reclining in a froth of surf,
loose hair swirling around bare
shoulders, my eyes half-closed

that's when I decided to move
to Toba City to learn to work
as a pearl diver on Pearl Island
for the Mikimoto Pearl Company

we dove there for Akoya oysters,
which perliculturers implanted
with the tiny grit of irritating nuclei,
making the oysters secrete layers
of nacre to grow a cultured pearl

then we hid the seeded oysters
in protected ledges within the seabed,
safe from typhoons and red tide

we performed for westerners
and tourists in modest white
cotton suits designed by Mikimoto,
and there was a kind of celebrity
in this that made us feel
temporarily, at least, a little
like American cinema stars

eventually, I married a fisherman

several decades later, Mikimoto
found a method of seeding pearls
more efficient than the old ways

and though tourists still come
to see diving on Pearl Island
it's no longer real, just a show,
like an image held still in time—
not of how things really are,
but of how things used to be

when my husband inherited
his older brother's fishing boat
in Kuji City, we moved back
to his childhood home and began
working on the Tohoku coast

though I'm an old woman now,
I dive every day, and each year
the *ama* and fish both dwindle

none of my daughters, or my
granddaughters or even my
great granddaughters, show
any desire to dive, and though
there have been women divers
since the ancient Nara era,
some people say we are
the last generation of *ama*

at 78, I'm one of the oldest,
but still, on most days I surface

with a catch of sea urchin
or octopus, possibly an abalone,
or sometimes even a coveted
horned turban-shell snail

I know the seabed better
than the creased geography
of lines that mapwork
my husband's weathered face,
and I've seen such strange
things beneath the surface:

a starfish whose legs tore off
of their own accord and walked
away, spilling out the insides

a wolf eel that sought me out
like a pet, letting me feed it
urchins and clams by hand

thousands of baby octopuses
like an exploding constellation
of slickly glittery rubber stars

when the tsunami struck,
at first I tried to outrun it
by seeking higher ground,
but when this seemed useless
I thought: *how stupid! why
should I run from the tide?*

so I turned around to face
the rising wall of curled surf,
so much more magnificent
more terrible than Hokusai's

then I made a final image
of my life to tie myself to
like a wooden buoy, took
one long deep breath, and dove
back into the sea again

kikuchi octopus

each of its eight arms can lift
up to 440 pounds to clear
radioactive debris and rubble

octopuses collect tchotchkes
and garland their eggs in their dens
on strings like twinkle lights

Doc Ock, the nuclear physicist
and Spiderman's arch-nemesis,
engineered radiation-proof tentacles
of immense strength and precision,
harnessing them to his body

sometimes octopuses will rip off
the stinging tentacles
from a Portugese man-of-war
to repurpose them as weapons

it comes with a laser attachment
that beams through stone,
a grappler to handle nuclear waste

a shy cephalopod of a child
with Coke bottle lens glasses,
Doc Ock was terrorized
by his brutally abusive father

a 100-pound pacific octopus
who wants to disappear
will squeeze through a hole
the size of a cherry tomato

it is all terrain, can remove fallen trees,
extinguish chemical fires

some octopuses are illusionists
who conjure up pseudomorphs—
life-size doppelgangers created
from a cloud of ink and mucous—
to act as a decoy to predators

Doc Ock becomes cyborg during
a nuclear accident—tentacles fused to
his body, brain rewired to manipulate
the prosthetics by Wi-Fi telepathy

octopuses can recognize human faces

emo tsunami

sometimes she's so lonely

she unscrews herself like a bolt
at 4:00 a.m.

from the jittery rhinestoned
terror of it

from the wasted life / cats will gnaw
the face from her skull
before the villagers
smell the smell of it

from the only an Ativan
can slow the oscillating
tornado siren in her chest
deafening the corn of it

from the only a second Ativan
can begin to smudge
the incriminating rusted-out edges
of the set stain of it

a menace of loneliness
luminous as a bare bulb
snapped on in the dark
false marigold and fire
to lost starships of moths

a menace of loneliness so hot
she could dustbuster
everyone / everything
into the slo-mo implosion
of her failed star's self:

a pogrom of beloveds
a covey of towhees
an escargatoire of sunflowers
a yoke of artichokes
a fluther of jellyfish
a bouquet of axolotls

a plump of cummerbunds
a wedge of polystyrene
an ostentation of aerosols
a lamentation of cloverleafs
a pride of skylines
a knob of nylon

a boil of decontaminants
a scourge of becquerels
a skein of gamma rays
a zeal of sieverts
an exaltation of protactinium
a husk of primordial nuclides

a half-life / of a half-life
a mean lifetime / of a mean lifetime

suicide pact / with the cosmos

be together / be together forever

we are stardust
we are molten
we are black holes

song of the mutant super boars

they are roving / the wild boars
on the move across farmlands
and main streets / trampling gardens
rooting through rubble / snuffling trash
looting noodle stands / nuzzling
the rotten stores of grocery markets
feral and mean and strong
left on their own to thrive
in the no go zone / plumped up
on radioactive plants and vermin
muscle and bone and fat / live
with the electric current of cesium 137
disco-glittering their veins
porkbelly shoulder chop and loin
still delicious but poisonous
to human predators who stay away
the way birds have learned to avoid
monarch caterpillars fattened
on noxious milkweed / all that
wasted radioactive flesh buried
in mass graves deep in the heart
of the no go zone until
there's no more room to go
encroaching into the yards
of abandoned homes / the fallow
corners of wrecked farms
where they're dug up and eaten
by packs of left-behind dogs

now radioactive dogs / a proper
cremation / at a safe burn facility
to keep radioactive particles
from leaking into the air only
possible at the rate of three
boars per day and there are
so many / thirteen thousand
running wild and unchecked / 200
pounds apiece of radioactive boars
bulldozing down the farmland
with glow-in-the-dark hooves
and contaminated snouts / mutant

super boars / new syndicate
of the no go zone / smarter
than charlotte / demagogues
of their own brutal animal farm
batteries invincible and energized
on 130 years of radioactive half life
stamping it down / all of it / the boars
will inherit / to tear it all down

hisako's testimony (as x-men's armor)

evacuees go home!
reads the graffiti in Iwaki,
but there's still no home
to go to in the no go zone

it's not like I ever asked
to come here and live
in this drafty prefab box
of corrugated metal
with my silent old granny

they call it temporary
but it's been two years

they call it housing
but it seems like a camp

both my parents died
in the tsunami, and granny
hasn't been the same
since we were evacuated

she lets me run wild
as the mangy starving cats,
as the feral rapeseed
and knotweed that weave
through the debris where

our house used to stand
on our property in Namie

I quit going to school

I dyed my hair bright blue
like a Harajuku girl
and got a secret tattoo
of the rabbit in the moon

my parents used to tell me
only second-class citizens
and gangsters had tattoos,

but everything's different now
and what can they say to me?

I think I wouldn't mind being
a moon rabbit gangster

or maybe a mutant superhero
like in the X-men anime

my favorite X-man is Armor
(a.k.a. Hisako Ichiki) because
(1) we are both named Hisako,
and (2) we are both fourteen

sometimes at night I used to
take a bus down to Iwaki's

entertainment district to see
the pretty bar hostesses
plying red-faced *sararimen*
amid the glittering arcades,
soba stalls, and pachinko parlors

there'd been rumors that
the transient population
of TEPCO cleanup workers
were turning Iwaki into
a rough and tumble man camp

at first, I thought this meant
there'd be more loud, gruff men
with unshaven faces than usual

but what surprised me most
was how young they were

some looked like country boys
starved for any work, away
from home for the first time

there were stories of thefts
and drunken street fights,
of people getting beaten
in dark alleyways at night

but I was a gangster moon rabbit!

faster than the tsunami

faster than any trouble I could find

he called to me from across
the street in a Kyushu dialect:
little blue-haired girl, he said,
can you show me the way
to the train station?

I hesitated, and he called out
to me again: *yes, I mean you,*
little blue-haired girl

something about the held-back
laughter in his voice almost
made me think of my father,
but up close I saw the flatness
in his eyes, smelled the stench
of whiskey and sweat, realizing
I'd made a terrible mistake

now I know why the feral cats
by the prefabs that I always try
to coax close enough to pet
run away from me instead

he punched me so hard
it set off a fizzle of sparks,

like a cascade of shaken
ginger ale behind my eyes

he dragged me into an alley
where he bound my wrists
with twine, stuffed a grubby
bandana into my mouth

in the X-men anime, after
Armor's been kidnapped
by the U-men, who try to steal
her organs, the X-men come
to Japan and rescue her

he raped and beat me behind
a dumpster, then showed me
his knife, said if I told anyone
he would find me and kill me

then he slit the twine
and ran away, and though
I was bruised and bleeding,
when I went to the police
to report it, the officer said
I shouldn't have been out
by myself so late at night

then he told me to go home

I don't know what granny
thought when she woke up
and came into the bathroom,
where I was trying to cry
as silently as possible, or if—
when she saw my black eyes,
my split lip, my torn clothes—
she believed the clumsy lie
I told her about falling down
the train station stairs

but she pried open my fingers,
quietly took the washrag away
and wrung it out in the basin
of cold water, then gently
dabbed my swollen face clean,
clucking her tongue each time
I winced from the sting

I wanted to tell her everything,
but felt too much shame

she's been so empty, vague,
and sad, how could I possibly
bear to upset her in this way?

I worry about granny so much,
because there've been suicides
among the elderly evacuees

sometimes the men hang
themselves, and sometimes
the women just stop eating

I always try to buy granny
sacks of oranges because
I know they're her favorite,
and I make sure to get
the safe-to-eat kind
from Hiroshima, even though
they're more expensive

oftentimes, I find she's lit
incense, and set the fruit out
on the altar that's centered
with my parents' pictures

Armor's superpower is a red,
impenetrable psionic exoskeleton.

it gives her superhuman strength
and makes her invulnerable

even the Muramasa blade
can't penetrate her armor

and if she feels fragile or upset,
her armor can expand to the size
of a giant space alien lizard

bigger than a city building . . .

bigger than the tsunami, even . . .

because her armor's smelted
from her ancestors' ghosts

because it's forged in memory

origin of tsunami

a cracked moon smithereened
on the porch room floor

broken mayonnaise jar's vinegary
infection fault-lining the basement

fractals of shattered wood
striking her into subjectivity

mothballed kimono's too-tight *obi*
binding her into compliance

picture frame that frames her
guilty accomplice in disguise / face
effaced behind a *ko-omote* mask

doll she shames / tortures in the attic
(hates its cracked helplessness)
(hates its broken imperfection)

afterward she feels sick
hides in the closet and cries

barbed wire that interns her

the shoes that pinch
the jeans that ride
the bra that chafes

gunpoint that coolly splays
and pins her into place

chloroformed lepidoptera / dangly carrot on a stick

the silver bar behind which lies
the perpetually withheld pellet

a hoop of flame licked / by a flickering whip

boy in a drunken rage
who smashes her face:
pulped lips / black eyes
her hair in his fist
head slammed hard
on the hardwood floor

(afterward he sets her best dress
on fire with his cigarette lighter)

vise clench of the hole / she's supposed to fill

the tiny hostage crawl space
into which she must try
to contain her shrilled edges
those monstrous feelings
her needy needs / shut the fuck up
sandbag them back
keep it all from vomiting out

landslide of gag rules shoved down her throat:

don't tell don't tell
don't rock the boat
shhhh / shhhh
don't make any waves

ghosts of the tohoku coast

of course, the ghosts are everywhere:

the face that blooms confused
in an unfurling peony bud

the dog that doesn't know it's dead
returning to search for the child
who used to pet and play with it

the fisherman who comes to shore
with early morning's neatly mended nets
looking for his small docked boat

taking taxi rides / wanting to go home
demanding to know: *am I still alive?*

oyurushi / oyurushi

whisked tea leaves whispering
from the bottom of a cup

the dancing funnel cloud of dust
that rises from a beaten futon

a murmuration of tiny gnats
helixing up like incense from
shriveled fruit at the broken altar

the jumble of unsortable bones
dustpanned out to sea

the husband / the wife
the mother / the daughter
the son / the father
the sister / the brother

all searching for what's been lost

driven by the electric pain
of phantom limbs
seizing up like dowsing rods

the grief of empty cicada shells
for what's been torn out trying
to fill themselves back up
with the transparency of rain

how many centuries will it take
for these stricken mists
and fogs to be burned away?

for this haunted water
to evaporate / to be exorcised
and rinsed clean again by light?

tsunami in love: kintsukuroi / golden joinery

> *When the Japanese mend broken objects, they aggrandize
> the damage by filling the cracks with gold. They believe
> that when something's suffered damage and has a history
> it becomes more beautiful.* —BARBARA BLOOM

safe is just another empty signifier
when she is water and the clay
that cupped her was a shattered bowl

triggering tsunami a sparkly blue shooter
pinging the splintered core
of the fractured nuclear reactor

this is what playing for keeps means
this broken imperfection / these cracked
masks / this crazed helplessness

this is what no going back means
no taking back the feral chipped singing
gouging open her fault lines and wounds

aggrandizing them with molten gold
blood veins of cinnabar alchemizing
to mercury like smelt silvering the shore

safe is just another empty signifier
because she is water and the clay
that cupped her was a shattered bowl

until after months in pieces she lets you
hold and rock her in these postures of repair
(and when she spills you do not drown

and when she rages in her radioactive
expansion cloud chamber you become
that slim umbilical tethering the astronaut

seaweed that fetters rafts of sea otters)
buttery lamp light by the side of the bed
gilding together what's broken no more

origami of tsunami: a technical manual and glossary

a

all clear: after she's swept it all
away / even the sirens

amplitude: the rising tide of her hips

arrival time: when she rolls up to your
door with seaweed salad
and fresh tofu in a bucket
/ a pulsing bouquet of
jellyfish bubbling like
Mylar balloons atop their
stingers and bristles /
ready to sweep you off
your feet

b

bathymetry: tsunami's background
check / her FBI file / her
origin myths / her
ground zero

bore: what she secretly thinks
of you and your
goody-two-shoes efforts

to salvage the world /
your heroic inspirational
speeches and your blah
blah blah / what she
thinks on the brink / of
unleashing tsunamigeddon

c

crest:
(consolidated reporting of
earthquakes and tsunamis)

spyware that tracks her
every point and
click / blue-gloved sack
and pillage of her luggage
at at the airport / her
seismic Foursquare / her
Facebook check-in

d

(empty)

e

eta:

slo-mo time-lapse
between bullet's impact
and psychological trigger /
arc between collision of

wants and teapot's
tempest sloshing / hard
line of the other shoe
dropping / nanosecond
between threat perceived
and the limbic's panicky
spill of adrenaline

evacuation zones: you you and you

f

first motion: trauma's urtext
free field offshore profile:
her glorious measurements
undiminished by corsets /
or girdles / or Dexedrine /
or Slim-fast / or Atkins /
or SlimVox / or AmbiSlim /
or Dietrine / or SlimQuick
Cleanse / or Stimuretix /
or Colonoxy / or Ayds

g

(empty)

h

harbor resonance:

shame spiral / negative
reaction formation's
fibonacci of nuclear
fission / negative thought
loop's slow gyre of
radioactive decay

horizontal inundation distance:

tsunami tries out for the
Olympics / maybe shot
put / maybe javelin /
possibly high jump / not
curling / not ribbon
twirling

i

icg/itsu:
(international coordination
group for the tsunami
warning system in the pacific)

tsunami's HMO sans Aflac

inundation:

tsunami's inbox / tsunami's
complaint box / your
box / how wet will it get?

itic:
(international tsunami
information center)

tsunami's human
resources file / tsunami's
bio / tsunami's CV /
tsunami on Wikipedia /
tsunami's Tumblr /
tsunami's exes

j

(empty)

k

(empty)

l

leading depression wave:

dead calm of dull leaden
sadness / chest pounding
open the hysterical night /
glimmer of Nova or Surfer
or Morg or Stardust or
some other shiny fleeting
nymph underneath 4:00
a.m.'s bedside light
heralding the arrival of
Galactus come to shove

	a straw deep inside her and suck her puny crumpling juice box dry
leading positive wave:	she turns and faces the threatening villagers with their flaming sticks / gives them the finger and drowns them / that'll show them / the end
local/regional tsunami:	sick day due to personal earthquake / mental health day due to psychic landslide

m

marigram:	allowable weight of emotional baggage
marigraph:	because size matters
mllw: (mean lower low water)	when tsunami's a bad drunk
ms: (surface wave magnitude)	second-wave tsunami

m_w:

her grandiosity / the
rising image of her false
(moment magnitude)
self / earthquake survival
strategies vis-à-vis
anachronistic coping
mechanisms such as
adopting the tsunami
posture etc.

n

noaa:
(national oceanic and
atmospheric administration)

tsunami's psychic hotline
shilled by her very own
Dionne Warwick look-
alike / her oracle / her
Japanese singing twins

nws:
(national weather service)

tsunami's publicist

o

(empty)

p

ptwc:
(pacific tsunami warning
center)

tsunami does the diaspora /
tsunami strikes back at
empire

period:

universal punctuation
between peak and trough /
Midol and hell /
uncontrollable weeping
held back tight behind
the eyes

p-wave:

tsunami's geek name

q

(empty)

r

runup:

tsunami's thug name

s

seiche:

tsunami's stripper name

sswws:
(seismic sea wave warning
system)

vodka and Ativan and
crying jags, o my!

strike-slip earthquake:

tsunami makes a
freudian slip and falls
into a vast vast canyon

s-wave:

tsunami's gangsta name

t

teletsunami:

her weekly hard-core
nature reality show taking
the globe by storm /
only! / on the Discovery! /
Channel!

thrust:
(the project for tsunami
hazard reduction using
system technology)

she dons a strap-on redux

thrust earthquake:

tsunami bottoms /
confuses thrust earthquake
for a trust earthquake

tidal wave:

tsunami's derby name

time:
(the center for the tsunami
inundation mapping effort)

age-defying tsunami /
prevents wrinkles and
fault lines / improves
elasticity / instant
hydration

tsunami earthquake:

the one that breaks her
heart

tsunamigenic earthquake:

the ones that craze it with
hairline fractures

tsunami evacuation maps:

in the mountains she
escapes from herself /
shape-shifts into a cloud /
French-exhaling sighs of
mist in relief / impresses
the mountain goats /
catastrophe averted

tsunami magnitude:

her fierceness / her
speedballed locomotion /
her hubris / the sashay of
her hips / the fatale of
her femme

tsunami watching:

toms lingering peepingly
outside her window / her
Facebook feed creepers

and clickers / adrenaline-
junkied tsunami chasers
on the Discovery Channel /
birders notebooking
tsunami sightings /
documenting her for
the rare ornithological
specimen that she is

tws: the sirens / the loud
(tsunami warning system)   speakers / the radioed
                                  meme

u

urgent tsunami warning: tsunamigeddon imminent

usnsn   tsunami's shrink / her
(united states national seismic   reiki healer / her guru /
network)   her Yoda / her primal
                                  scream institute

v

(empty)

w

wc/atwc:
(west coast/alaska tsunami
warning center)

tsunami cruises through
Alaska / a supposedly
fun thing she'll never do
again

wrap around effect:

the ouroboros of her
terrible radiance

x

(empty)

y

(empty)

z

(empty)

acknowledgments

Versions of these works have appeared in the following journals and anthologies:

The Account—"kikuchi octopus" and "year of the hitachi snake"
Alaska Quarterly Review—"ghosts of the tohoku coast"
American Poetry Review—"emo tsunami," "dreaming tsunami," and "origin of tsunami"
burntdistrict—"animal portents foretell the rise of tsunami" and "shapeshifter tsunami: a scary epithalamium"
Cobalt—"beautiful tsunami"
diode—"ama, the woman of the sea," "hungry tsunami / tsunami as galactus," "mothra flies again," "tsunami's debris," "origami of tsunami: a technical manual and glossary," and "white tsubame"
Eye to the Telescope (Asian American Speculative Poetry Issue)—"ontology of tsunami"
The Feminist Wire—"tsunami battles the pink robots / french poststructuralist tsunami" (as: "tsunami vs. the pink hitachi robots / poststructuralist tsunami") and "tsunami grrlsplains allergies"
Indiana Review—"radioactive man"
The Margins (Asian American Writer's Workshop)—"miki endo as flint marko (a.k.a. sandman)"
Motionpoems—"song of the mutant super boars"
North Dakota Quarterly—"anonymous, as invisible man"

Poetry Crush—"tsunami in love: kintsukuroi / golden joinery"
Sugar House Review—"hisako's testimony (as x-men's armor)," "hulk smash," "tsunami goes to canada," and "tsunami as misguided kwannon"

"origin of tsunami" reprinted in *Wingbeats II: Exercises and Practice in Poetry*. Eds. Scott Wiggerman and David Meischen. Austin: Dos Gatos Press, 2014.
"tsunami battles the pink robots / french poststructuralist tsunami" (as: "tsunami vs. the pink hitachi robots / poststructuralist tsunami") and "tsunami grrlsplains allergies" reprinted in *Political Punch: Contemporary Poems on the Politics of Identity*. Eds. Fox Frazier-Foley and Erin Elizabeth Smith. Knoxville: Sundress Publications, 2016.

I would also like to thank Hedgebrook, Willapa Bay AiR, the Women's International Study Center at Acequia Madre House, the Bunnell Street Arts Center, the South Dakota Arts Council, the Banff Centre for Arts and Creativity, the Kimmel Harding Nelson Center for the Arts, and the University of South Dakota, for the gifts of funding, time, space, and support without which this book would not be possible.

Cathy Flum

LEE ANN RORIPAUGH is the author of four previous collections of poems. Her first collection, *Beyond Heart Mountain*, was selected by Ishmael Reed as a National Poetry Series winner. Her second, *Year of the Snake*, was named winner of the Association of Asian American Studies Book Award. Her third book, *On the Cusp of a Dangerous Year*, was lauded as "masterful" and a "gorgeous canticle" (Maura Stanton). Most recently, her fourth collection of poems, *Dandarians*, was described as "a work of beauty and resilience" (Srikanth Reddy). Roripaugh has received an Archibald Bush Foundation Artist Fellowship, the Frederick Manfred Award from the Western Literature Association, the Randall Jarrell International Poetry Prize, and an Academy of American Poets Prize. She serves as Editor-in-Chief of *South Dakota Review* and directs the creative writing program at the University of South Dakota, as well as being the state's Poet Laureate. She resides in Vermillion.

milkweed
editions

Founded as a nonprofit organization in 1980,
Milkweed Editions is an independent publisher.
Our mission is to identify, nurture and publish
transformative literature, and build an engaged
community around it.

milkweed.org

Interior design by Mary Austin Speaker
Typeset in Bembo

Bembo was created in the 1920s under the
direction of printing historian Stanley Morison for
the Monotype Corporation. Bembo is based upon the
1495 design cut by Francesco Griffo for Aldus Manutius,
and named after the first book to use the typeface,
a small book called *De Aetna*, by the Italian
poet and cleric Pietro Bembo.